FINDING HOME

WORDS FROM KIDS SEEKING SANCTUARY

By Gwen Agna and Shelley Rotner | Photographs by Shelley Rotner

Clarion Books
An Imprint of HarperCollinsPublishers

Kids from all over the world have to leave their homes and countries.

They have to escape—
fleeing fires, floods, drought, or war—
because it's not safe for them to stay anymore.

Many families leave hoping to find freedom,
a better life—**a new home**.

Families belong together.

Most people had to travel for a long time—months, even years, moving from place to place before finally finding a new home.

It was hard to make friends at first when you speak a different language.

I couldn't understand **them**, and they couldn't understand **me**.

It takes a lot of courage—you have to be brave to move somewhere new.

Everything was **new** and **different**.

Here we have recess.
Yes!

Let's hope for a world

where everyone is welcome.

More About the Journeys to Finding a New Home

At first we thought we heard something like a helicopter. But when we heard the noise again, we knew they were bombing us. We grabbed our backpacks and could take only what we could carry. We all ran as fast as we could to my uncle's house because he had a car. We piled in and kept driving until we got to Poland. From Poland to France. From France to Canada, and then to the United States. A lot of us are together and we're with our cousins who already lived here, but some family got left behind.

We finally got onto a plane in Afghanistan after walking for two days with very little food or water. First, we landed and stayed in Qatar, an Arab country. Then we went to Germany for a while. Then to refugee camps in the United States—in Indiana and Virginia—and now our home is in Massachusetts.

It was my first time ever being on a plane. It was exciting at first, then a relief, and then we all went to sleep because we were so tired and woke up somewhere else.

First, we got to Romania, then Germany, then Cancun, and then Tijuana, where they put us in cells for days. It was like a jail. We finally were let out and we crossed the border to San Diego. Then we flew across the country to where our cousins lived. We've been here for two months now, but all of us are still exhausted.

I want my new friends to know that building trust is the most important thing. Be good to the people who care about you.

For Children:
How to Help Welcome Someone New

Imagine what it would feel like to move to a new country, to a new home, and to make new friends and learn a new language. Any kind gestures would be welcoming. And you might even make a new friend!

HELPFUL TIPS:

- Try to be friendly. Show how happy you are by smiling! You may not speak the same language, but smiles need no translation.
- Practice how to say "hello" and "it's nice to meet you" in other languages than your own. A grown-up can help you use Google Translate.
- Be welcoming toward each other, whether in the classroom or at the playground, by playing games or by doing things you both like.
- Please remember to be patient and understanding, and to respect that some kids may be shy and afraid to join in.

How Can Grown-Ups Help?

THERAPEUTIC ADVICE

Every resettling child is unique, shaped by family, culture, race, beliefs, and social or political context. What all resettling children share is the experience of dislocation, loss, and immersion in the unfamiliar, as well as a history that their new neighbors may well have little way of understanding or imagining. Many children struggle with memories of witnessing or experiencing terrifying violence in their home countries. These experiences of trauma may be spoken of freely by a child, or may persist hiddenly as puzzling behaviors and eruptions of intense feelings. As they learn a new language and culture, some children carry deep fears, sadness, and hurt that complicate their entry into their new lives. Healing can take time.

Beyond the basics of a secure home and economic stability, what helps a child resettle in a new land? What contributes to the sense of safety that is essential to the processes of settling as well as healing? Seeing that their parents are coping and available emotionally even in the midst of so much change is critical. Parents and adult relatives need as much support as possible in resettling for their own well-being and also their children's. Children are helped by predictable routines and structure, which ground them in daily life. Forging strong connections to caring adults and new friends smooths the transition to a new and strange culture. Schools, community programs, and faith-based organizations that go out of their way to welcome and learn about (and from) their new neighbors make all the difference to children of all ages tasked with resettling.

Grown-ups who wish to welcome children and families resettling in their communities can reach out with warmth, kindness, and humility toward all that they may not understand as well as with excitement for all that they can learn from their new neighbors. We can provide crucial supports that strengthen children's parents as they navigate raising children in a strange land. And we can make sure that all children's gifts and passions are truly seen and nurtured in their new communities.

—Cynthia Monahon, Psy.D., *licensed clinical psychologist specializing in displaced families*

More Ways to Help for Parents, Caregivers, and Educators

Today, more than 100 million people, half of whom are children, have been forced to leave their homes. There is great instability all over the world, mostly due to climate change and political strife. We can help by encouraging people to support and welcome refugees new to our communities by modeling kindness, generosity, and understanding.

Here are some practical ways to help recommended by the office of the United Nations High Commissioner for Refugees (UNHCR.org).

- Volunteer with an organization for people seeking asylum near you. You could offer to teach a language, craft, or sport.
- Navigate and help complete the paperwork for medical and government services.
- Help with job searching and support businesses run by displaced people. Hire them for jobs if you are in a position to do so.
- Offer training or volunteer opportunities.
- Become a supporter and advocate! Join a campaign that raises awareness about refugee issues and shows solidarity.
- Help people feel at home. Be a tour guide in your community; invite refugees to activities like sporting events, fairs, or public library programs; or share a meal.
- Donate. It might not feel very hands-on to you, but your donation will make a difference in people's lives.

A one-time donation by the publisher has been made to the UNHRC.

Authors' Notes

Gwen: As a longtime elementary school principal, I have led a school that over the years has welcomed children from Kosovo, Bosnia, and Congo. I know firsthand the trauma, disruption, and grief they experience. I also have seen what gifts they bring to a community of learners. Perhaps most importantly, I want to recognize the power of picture books—for all ages—in supporting and educating children, families, and educators in the process of making a new home. We would like to acknowledge that we have immense respect for these families. It is our intention to promote empathy and love for those who have been displaced and are trying to find a new home.

Shelley: As a nonfiction author, photo-illustrator, and photojournalist I was privileged to get to know and work with the many families settling where I live. It was my intention to help build bridges welcoming them as they navigated a new home, and to give them a place to be seen, heard, and represented as valued humans. Although experiencing extreme trauma and change, both culturally and with language barriers, these families shared a universal thread of kindness and graciousness. It was a gift for me to share the children's joy in discovering a playground, playing on a grass soccer field, or going to school and making new friends—just being kids. I want to thank everyone for their bravery and courage, and for trusting me.

Additional Resources

REFUGEE CHILDREN'S HEALTH AND MENTAL HEALTH

fugeesfamily.org
Fugees Family is a trauma-informed approach for refugee and newcomer students based on holistic English acquisition, integration of athletics, and year-round programming.

www.brycs.org
Bridging Refugee Youth and Children's Services works to empower and ensure the successful development of refugee children, youth, and their families.

SOCIAL SKILLS PROGRAMS

www.cfchildren.org
The Committee of Children promotes and implements research-based programs for the safety, well-being, and success of children by working with educators, parents, and policymakers.

www.refugees.org
The US Committee for Refugees builds bridges between new Americans and their communities through honoring

similarities, sharing and celebrating different cultures, humanizing people, and giving them a voice.

www.jewishfamilyservice.org
Jewish Family Services promotes diversity, equity, inclusion, and accessibility to help people of all ages and backgrounds achieve their goals, enhance their well-being, and increase their independence.

EDUCATIONAL MATERIALS

www.amnestyusa.org
Amnesty International produces educational material to inform people about human rights.

www.ccwny.org
Catholic Charities has education and employment programs for people sixteen and older that offer high school equivalency instruction, reading and math skills, tutoring, scheduling assistance, college prep, and translators.

www.unhcr.org/teaching-about-refugees.html
Teaching About Refugees provides

teaching materials on refugees, asylum, and migration for primary and secondary education and offers guidance for teachers working with refugee children in the classroom.

BOOKS FOR YOUR FAMILY LIBRARY

All Are Welcome, by Alexandra Penfold

From Far Away, by Robert Munsch

Stepping Stones: A Refugee Family's Journey, by Margaret Ruurs

The Journey, by Francesca Sanna

What Is a Refugee, by Elise Gravel

Why Do They Have to Fight? Refugee Children's Stories from Bosnia, Kurdistan, Somalia, and Sri Lanka, by Jill Rutter and Mano Candappa

Who Belongs Here? An American Story, by Margy Burns Knight

Glossary

Asylum—the protection granted by a nation to someone who has left their native country as a political refugee.

Border—an imaginary line separating two political or geographical areas. There are borders between countries, between states, and even between cities.

Citizenship—the position or status of being a citizen of a particular country.

Civil rights—the equal rights of citizens to political and social freedoms, as defined by the government of the community in which they hold citizenship.

Compassion—sympathy for someone else's distress and a desire to make them feel better.

Displaced person—a person who is forced to leave their home, typically because of war, persecution, or natural disaster.

Empathy—the ability to understand and share the feelings of another.

Émigré—a person who has left their own country in order to settle in another, typically for political reasons.

Integration—the process of mixing together or combining different groups of people into a single, unified body.

Migrant—a person who moves from one place to another, especially in order to find work or better living conditions.

Refuge—something or someplace that provides safety or shelter from pursuit, danger, or trouble.

Refugee—the political status given to a person forced to leave their country out of fear in order to escape war, persecution, or natural disasters like famine, flooding, drought, or fire.

Refugee camp—a settlement or encampment to house displaced people who have fled their home countries.

Resettle—to move people to a new place to live because they couldn't stay where they were.

Sanctuary—a place of refuge or safety.

Settlement—a place, typically one that has previously been uninhabited, where people establish a community.

We dedicate this book to courageous families and kids who come from all over the world—Afghanistan, Eritrea, Ethiopia, Haiti, Bosnia, Tibet, the Republic of Congo, South Sudan, Mexico, South America, Syria, Nigeria, Myanmar, and Ukraine— and who are settling into their new homes.

—*G. A. and S. R.*

Acknowledgments

We'd like to give special thanks to our inspirational and collaborative team:

Our agent, Liz Nealon, founder of Great Dog Literary, who has guided the way.

Our editor, Chris Krones, at Clarion Books, who believed in our vision that children should be seen and their voices heard.

Our book designer, Stephanie Hays, who created our vision for the world to see.

The photographs and quotes in our book were captured at a moment in time. We understand the danger that some of them have faced in their journeys, and the dangers people left behind still face, so we honor and protect all by not identifying anyone by name.

Clarion Books is an imprint of HarperCollins Publishers.
Finding Home: Words from Kids Seeking Sanctuary
Text copyright © 2024 by Gwen Agna and Shelley Rotner
Photographs copyright © 2024 by Shelley Rotner
All rights reserved. Manufactured in Italy. No part of this book may be used or reproduced in any manner whatsoever without written permission except in the case of brief quotations embodied in critical articles and reviews. For information address HarperCollins Children's Books, a division of HarperCollins Publishers, 195 Broadway, New York, NY 10007.
www.harpercollinschildrens.com

Library of Congress Control Number: 2022058361

ISBN 978-0-06-330417-8

Typography by Stephanie Hays & Lori Malkin Ehrlich

23 24 25 26 27 RTLO 10 9 8 7 6 5 4 3 2 1

First Edition